Contents

目次

本書の利用法
06

クマとミツバチ
The Bear and the Bees
09

キツネとネコ
The Fox and the Cat
15

ヒツジの皮をかぶったオオカミ
A Wolf in Sheep's Clothing
21

キツネと
ツル *The Fox and the Crane*
27

ウサギと
カメ *The Tortoise and the Hare*
33

アリと
ハト *The Ant and the Dove*
39

ロバと
イヌ *The Donkey and the Dog*
45

都会のネズミと
田舎のネズミ
The City Mouse and the Country Mouse
51

サソリと
カエル *The Scorpion and the Frog*
57

アリとキリギリス *The Ant and the Grasshopper* ... 63

踊るおサルさん *The Dancing Monkeys* ... 69

農夫の娘 *The Farmer's Daughter* ... 75

男と少年とロバ *The Man, the Boy, and the Donkey* ... 81

めすライオン *The Lioness* ... 87

農夫とヤギ *The Farmer and the Goats* ... 93

オオカミ少年
The Boy Who Cried Wolf
99

魔法使いと金の傘
The Wizard and the Gold Umbrella
105

王様と2人のお妃
The King and His Two Wives
111

ライオンとネズミ
The Lion and the Mouse

117

アヒルと金の卵
The Goose and the Golden Eggs
123

Index
129

本書の利用法

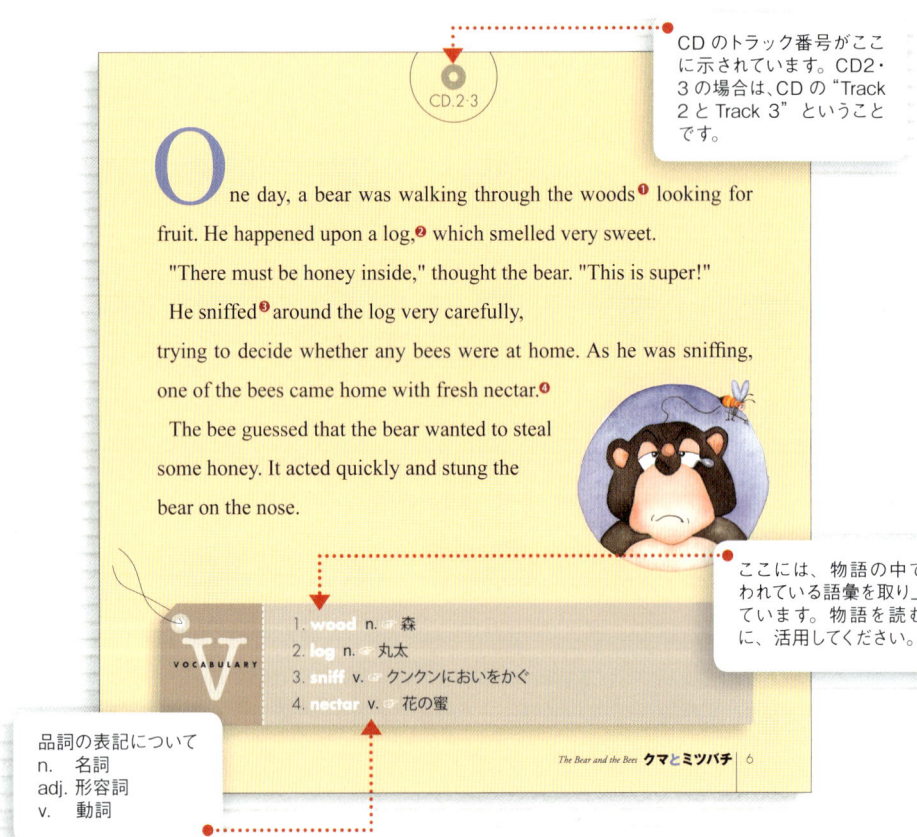

CDのトラック番号がここに示されています。CD2・3の場合は、CDの "Track 2 と Track 3" ということです。

One day, a bear was walking through the woods❶ looking for fruit. He happened upon a log,❷ which smelled very sweet.

"There must be honey inside," thought the bear. "This is super!"

He sniffed❸ around the log very carefully, trying to decide whether any bees were at home. As he was sniffing, one of the bees came home with fresh nectar.❹

The bee guessed that the bear wanted to steal some honey. It acted quickly and stung the bear on the nose.

VOCABULARY

1. **wood** n. 森
2. **log** n. 丸太
3. **sniff** v. クンクンにおいをかぐ
4. **nectar** v. 花の蜜

ここには、物語の中で使われている語彙を取り上げています。物語を読む際に、活用してください。

品詞の表記について
n. 名詞
adj. 形容詞
v. 動詞

The Bear and the Bees **クマとミツバチ** | 6

▶ **本書は、誰もが知っているお話を含めた20のイソップ物語が収録されています。
1つのお話はイラスト、日本語訳を含めて6ページで構成されており、
手軽に読み進めることができます。**

各お話の最後には日本語訳が載っています。日本語だけを読んでも自然なように、英語を翻訳したものもありますので、必ずしもVocabularyで紹介された意味と一致するとは限りません。

The Bear and the Bees

訳：クマとミツバチ

　ある日、一頭のクマが、果物を探しながら森の中を歩いていました。
　すると偶然、とても甘い香りのする丸太を見つけました。
「中にはハチミツが入っているに違いない」
　クマは考えました。
「これはいいぞ！」
　クマは、ハチがいないか確かめようと、丸太を注意深く嗅ぎ回ります。鼻をクンクンさせていると、一匹のハチが新鮮な花の蜜とともに帰ってきました。
　クマがハチミツを盗もうとしているんだと考えたハチは、素早く動くと、クマの鼻の上を刺しました。

　クマは、すぐにかっとなって丸太に飛び乗り、その大きな手でハチを叩きました。
「おまえたちみんなこらしめてやる！」
　クマはうなり声を上げました。
　すると丸太の中にいたハチたちがすべて出てきて、クマを攻撃しました。至るところをこれでもかと刺します。かわいそうなクマは逃げましたが、ハチたちはどこまでも追いかけてきます。ついにクマは逃れるために川に飛び込むしかなくなりました。
「やっとわかったよ」
　クマは言いました。
「ときには、戦うより、立ち去ったほうがいいんだな」

▶ 【ことわざ】「触らぬ神に祟りなし」

必要なものには、対応する日本のことわざを紹介しています。

学習法

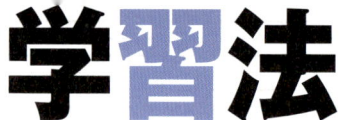

本書を使って英語の読解力や聴解力をアップさせるのに有効な学習法を紹介します。
お話を楽しみながら、英語力を上げるのに役立ててください。

Step1

Vocabularyをヒントにしながら物語を**読む**

Step2

日本語訳で**確認**

Step3

CD（英語）を本を**見ながら**聞く

Step4

CD（英語）を本を**見ないで**聞く

CD.2·3

偶数トラックには英語で、奇数トラックには日本語で、
お話が収録されています。
用途に合わせて、CDを活用してください。

The Bear and the Bees
クマとミツバチ

One day, a bear was walking through the woods[1] looking for fruit. He happened upon a log,[2] which smelled very sweet.

"There must be honey inside," thought the bear. "This is super!"

He sniffed[3] around the log very carefully, trying to decide whether any bees were at home. As he was sniffing, one of the bees came home with fresh nectar.[4]

The bee guessed that the bear wanted to steal some honey. It acted quickly and stung the bear on the nose.

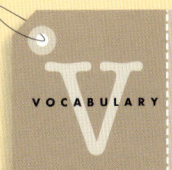

1. **wood** n. ☞ 森
2. **log** n. ☞ 丸太
3. **sniff** v. ☞ クンクンにおいをかぐ
4. **nectar** v. ☞ 花の蜜

The Bear and the Bees **クマとミツバチ**

The bear lost his temper❶ in an instant. He jumped on the log and beat❷ it with his large paws. "I will punish❸ all of you!" he roared.❹

Now all the bees inside the log came out and attacked the bear. They stung him over and over again. The poor bear ran away, but the bees chased him everywhere. Finally, the bear had to jump into a river to get away.

"Now I know," said the bear. "Sometimes it's better to walk away than to fight."

VOCABULARY

1. **temper** n. ☞ 気分
2. **beat** v. (beat-beat-beaten) ☞ たたく
3. **punish** v. ☞ こらしめる
4. **roar** v. ☞ うなる

The Bear and the Bees

訳：クマとミツバチ

　ある日、一頭のクマが、果物を探しながら森の中を歩いていました。
　すると偶然、とても甘い香りのする丸太を見つけました。
「中にはハチミツが入っているに違いない」
クマは考えました。
「これはいいぞ！」
　クマは、ハチがいないか確かめようと、丸太を注意深く嗅ぎ回ります。鼻をクンクンさせていると、一匹のハチが新鮮な花の蜜とともに帰ってきました。
　クマがハチミツを盗もうとしているんだと考えたハチは、素早く動くと、クマの鼻の上を刺しました。

　クマは、すぐにかっとなって丸太に飛び乗り、その大きな手でハチを叩きました。
「おまえたちみんなこらしめてやる！」
　クマはうなり声を上げました。
　すると丸太の中にいたハチたちがすべて出てきて、クマを攻撃しました。至るところをこれでもかと刺します。かわいそうなクマは逃げましたが、ハチたちはどこまでも追いかけてきます。ついにクマは逃れるために川に飛び込むしかなくなりました。
　「やっとわかったよ」
　クマは言いました。
「ときには、戦うより、立ち去ったほうがいいんだな」

【ことわざ】「触らぬ神に祟りなし」

The Fox and the Cat
キツネとネコ

One day, a fox and a cat were talking. The fox was very proud.❶ "I am very sly,"❷ he said.

"You are?" asked the cat.

"Yes," said the fox. "No one can catch me. I have a whole bag of tricks. I know a hundred ways to escape❸ from dogs and people."

The fox looked proudly at the cat. "How about you?"

The cat said quietly, "I have only one way, but that is usually enough."

After the cat said this, they heard a noise. It became louder and louder. The fox and the cat looked at each other.

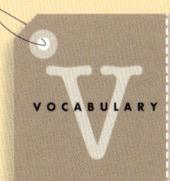

1. **proud** adj. ☞ 自慢している、高慢な
2. **sly** adj. ☞ ずる賢い
3. **escape** v. ☞ 逃げる

Suddenly, a pack of ❶ dogs ran toward the fox and the cat. Quickly, the cat ran up a tree and hid❷ behind some leaves. "This is my way to escape," he said. "What do you do?"

The fox thought about one way and then another. Some ways were better than other ways. Some ways might look good to the cat.

But as the fox thought it over, the dogs came nearer and caught him. The hunters and the dogs quickly killed the fox.

The cat thought, "Sometimes one is better than many."

VOCABULARY

1. **pack of~**　☞　〜の群れ
2. **hide**　v. (hide-hid-hidden)　☞　隠れる

The Fox and the Cat **キツネとネコ** | 19

訳：キツネとネコ

　ある日、キツネとネコが話をしていました。キツネはとても自慢屋です。
「僕はとっても賢いんだ」と言いました。
　「君が?」とネコはたずねます。
　「そうだとも」　キツネは言いました。
「誰も僕のことを捕まえられない。僕にはあらゆる手段がある。イヌと人間から逃れる方法を100通りも知ってるんだぜ」
　キツネは自慢げにネコを見ました。
「君は?」
　ネコは静かに言いました。
「僕は一つだけ。でも、たいていこれで十分だよ」
　ネコがこう言うと、物音が聞こえてきました。音はどんどん大きくなります。キツネとネコは顔を見合わせました。

　突然、イヌの群れがキツネとネコに向かって突進してきました。
　すぐにネコは木の上に駆け上がり、葉の陰に隠れました。
「これが僕の逃げる方法さ」とネコは言います。
「君はどうするの?」
　キツネは次々と方法を考えます。あの方法よりいい方法がある。あれはネコにいいかもしれない。
　でも、キツネが考えを巡らせている間に、イヌたちは近づいてきて、キツネをつかまえ、ハンターとイヌは素早くキツネを仕留めてしまいました。
　ネコは思いました。
「ときには数が多いより一つのほうがいいこともあるんだな」

A Wolf in Sheep's Clothing

ヒツジの皮をかぶったオオカミ

Once upon a time,❶ a wolf wanted to catch some sheep, but the shepherd❷ and his dogs were too careful. The wolf could not get near the sheep.

After a few days, the wolf sat on a hill❸ and looked at the sheep. One of the dogs walked over and said, "You will not catch our sheep. Dogs are too smart."

The wolf said, "Wolves are dogs, too, but wolves are smarter. You will see that when I catch a sheep."

Later, the wolf found a sheepskin❹ by the road, and he thought of a plan.

VOCABULARY

1. **once upon a time** ☞ 昔々のこと
2. **shepherd** n. ☞ 羊飼い
3. **hill** n. ☞ 丘
4. **sheepskin** n. ☞ 羊皮

A Wolf in Sheep's Clothing **ヒツジの皮をかぶったオオカミ**

The next day, the wolf dressed ❶in the sheepskin and walked into the field ❷with the sheep.

He walked around and no one knew he was a wolf. He looked at the dogs and thought, "Who is smarter? I am!"

Suddenly, the shepherd walked into the field to kill a sheep for meat. The wolf looked so much like a sheep that the shepherd killed him, and not a real ❸sheep.

When the shepherd picked up the sheepskin, he and the dogs saw it was the wolf. One of the dogs thought, "If you look for trouble, you will find it."

VOCABULARY

1. **dress** v. ☞ 着る
2. **field** n. ☞ 牧草地
3. **real** adj. ☞ 本物の

A Wolf in Sheep's Clothing **ヒツジの皮をかぶったオオカミ**

訳：ヒツジの皮をかぶったオオカミ

　昔々のこと。オオカミはヒツジを捕まえたいと思っていました。でも、羊飼いとそのイヌたちが用心深く、オオカミはヒツジたちに近づくことができません。
　数日後、オオカミは丘の上に腰を下ろし、ヒツジたちを見ていました。一匹のイヌが近づいてきて言います。
「ヒツジを捕まえることはできないよ。僕たちイヌはとても賢いからね」
　オオカミは言いました。
「オオカミだってイヌなんだぜ。でも、オオカミのほうがもっと賢いさ。オレがヒツジを捕まえたら、わかるってもんさ」
　その後、オオカミは道端でヒツジの皮を見つけました。そしてある計画を考えつきます。

　翌日、オオカミはヒツジの皮をかぶり、ヒツジたちに混じって牧草地に入り込みました。
　オオカミは歩き回りましたが、誰も自分がオオカミだと気付きません。イヌたちを見て思いました。
「どっちが賢いかって？　オレだよ！」
　すると突然、羊飼いが牧草地に歩いてきました。食用に一匹のヒツジを殺すためです。オオカミは、ヒツジそっくりに見えたので、羊飼いはオオカミを殺してしまいました。本当のヒツジではないのに。
　羊飼いがヒツジの皮をはいだとき、羊飼いとイヌたちはそれがオオカミであることに気付きました。一匹のイヌは思いました。
「トラブルは、いつでも起こりうるものなんだな」

The Fox and the Crane
キツネとツル

There once was a fox who lived alone in the forest. One day he was bored, so he invited the crane to dinner.

"Thanks," said the crane, who was very kind. "I accept your invitation!" ❶

At dinner, the crane was disappointed.❷ The fox served nothing but soup. He put it in big, flat dishes, and the crane couldn't eat it. The soup kept falling out of her long bill.❸ The fox laughed.

"You look so silly!" he said as he lapped up❹ his own soup.

1. **invitation** n. ☞ 招待
2. **disappointed** adj. ☞ がっかりした
3. **bill** n. ☞ くちばし
4. **lap up** v. ☞ 〜をごくごくと飲む

"My friend," said the crane, "thank you for dinner. Why don't you be my guest tomorrow? I make excellent soup."

"Sure," replied the fox, "I always welcome ❶ a free ❷ meal."

The next day, the crane made some delicious vegetable soup. The lovely smell made the fox's stomach growl.❸ However, when he sat down to eat, he couldn't. The crane had served the soup in tall cups. The fox's mouth couldn't reach the soup inside.

"I won't apologize ❹ for this dinner," said the crane, "for as everyone knows, one bad turn deserves another."

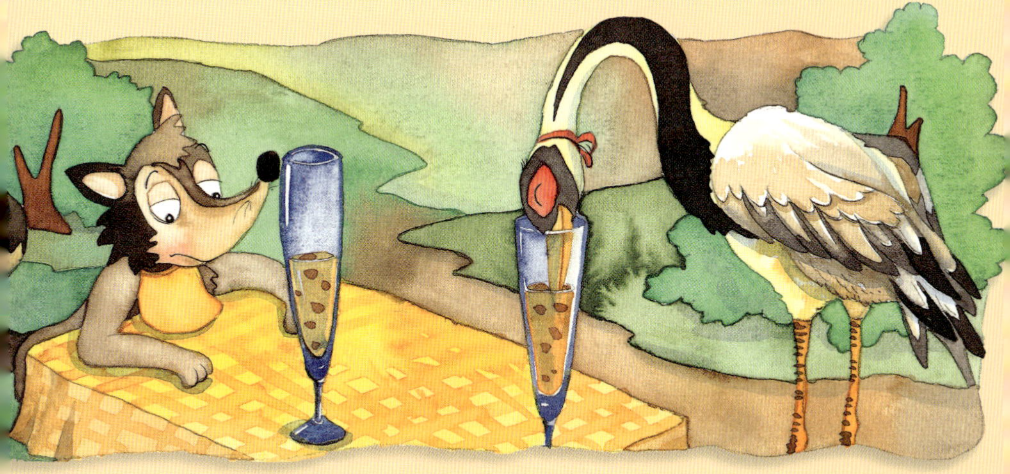

1. **welcome** v. ☞ 歓迎する
2. **free** adj. ☞ タダの
3. **growl** v. ☞ （お腹が）ぐーぐー鳴る
4. **apologize** v. ☞ あやまる

訳：キツネとツル

　昔々、森の中にキツネが一匹で暮らしていました。ある日、退屈したキツネは、ツルを夕食に招きました。
　「ありがとう」　心のやさしいツルは言いました。
「喜んでうかがいますよ！」
　夕食のとき、ツルはがっかりしました。キツネが用意したのはスープだけ。キツネはスープを大きな平たい皿に盛ったので、ツルは飲むことができなかったのです。スープは、ツルの長いくちばしからはこぼれてしまいます。キツネは笑いました。
　「間抜けな姿だな！」
　キツネは自分のスープをごくごく飲みながら、そう言いました。

　「キツネさん」　ツルは言いました。
「夕食をありがとう。明日は、私のところにいらっしゃらない？ おいしいスープをごちそうするわ」
　「もちろん」　キツネは答えました。
「ただ飯ならいつでも歓迎さ」
　翌日、ツルはおいしい野菜スープを作りました。おいしそうな匂いに、キツネのお腹がグルルと鳴りました。でも、テーブルについても、キツネは食べることができませんでした。ツルはスープを背の高いカップに注いだからです。キツネの口は、中にあるスープに届きません。
　「食事のこと、私はあやまりませんよ」　ツルは言いました。
「意地悪をしたら同じ目に遭う。みんな知っていることですから」

The Tortoise and the Hare
ウサギとカメ

One day, the hare❶ told some other animals that he could run fast. He said, "I have never lost a race.❷ I will race anyone."

Then the hare looked at the tortoise ❸ and laughed. He said that the tortoise had short legs and was very slow.

The tortoise said, "I will race you."

The hare was surprised and laughed more. "I can dance around you."

"Yes," said the tortoise. "You are as swift as the wind, but I will win."

The hare thought this was impossible❹ and said OK. They agreed on a day and a place, and all the other animals talked about the race.

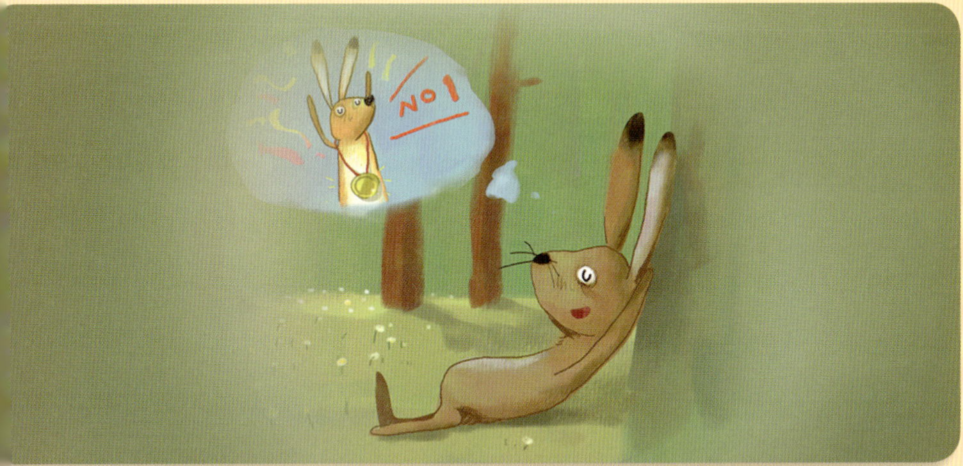

VOCABULARY

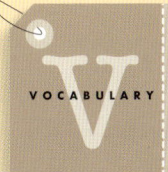

1. **hare** n. ☞ 野ウサギ
2. **race** ☞ 競争 (n.)、競争する (v.)
3. **tortoise** n. ☞ カメ
4. **impossible** adj. ☞ 不可能な、ありえない

On the day of the race, all the animals came to watch. The race began. The tortoise started walking slowly but surely. The hare quickly ran out of sight.

Another animal might stop and give up, but not the tortoise. The tortoise continued ❶ walking.

Then the hare stopped. He was confident ❷ that he would beat the tortoise, so he lay down and took a nap.❸

The tortoise continued walking and walking.

When the hare woke up, he saw that the tortoise had won the race and was resting under a tree.

The tortoise said to the hare, "Slowly but surely wins the race."

VOCABULARY

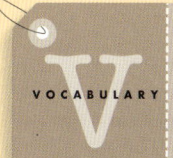

1. **continue** v. ☞ 続ける
2. **confident** adj. ☞ 自信がある
3. **nap** n. ☞ 昼寝

The Tortoise and the Hare **ウサギとカメ**

訳：ウサギとカメ

　ある日、野ウサギは、動物たちに向かって自分は速く走れると言いました。野ウサギは言います。
「僕は絶対に負けたことがない。誰とだって競走するよ」
　そして野ウサギは、リクガメを見て笑いました。野ウサギは、リクガメの足は短く、歩みがノロいと言います。リクガメは言いました。
「競走しようよ」
　野ウサギはびっくり。そして大笑いしました。
「君の周りでダンスしてあげるよ」
「そうだね」
　リクガメは言いました。
「君は風のように速い。でも、勝つのは僕さ」
　野ウサギは、それはあり得ないと思い、承諾しました。日にちと場所が決まると、ほかの動物たちはレースのことをうわさしました。

　当日、動物たちはみんな見学に訪れました。競走のスタートです。リクガメはゆっくりと、でも着実に歩き始めました。野ウサギは、早くも視界から消えてゆきました。
　ほかの動物だったら、立ち止まり、あきらめてしまったかもしれません。でも、リクガメは違いました。歩き続けたのです。
　一方、野ウサギは立ち止まりました。リクガメに勝てると確信した野ウサギは、横になって昼寝をしました。
　リクガメはひたすら歩き続けました。
　目を覚ました野ウサギが見たのは、リクガメが競走に勝って、木の下で休んでいる光景でした。
　リクガメは野ウサギに言いました。
「ゆっくりでも着実に歩む者が競争に勝つんだよ」

The Ant and the Dove
アリとハト

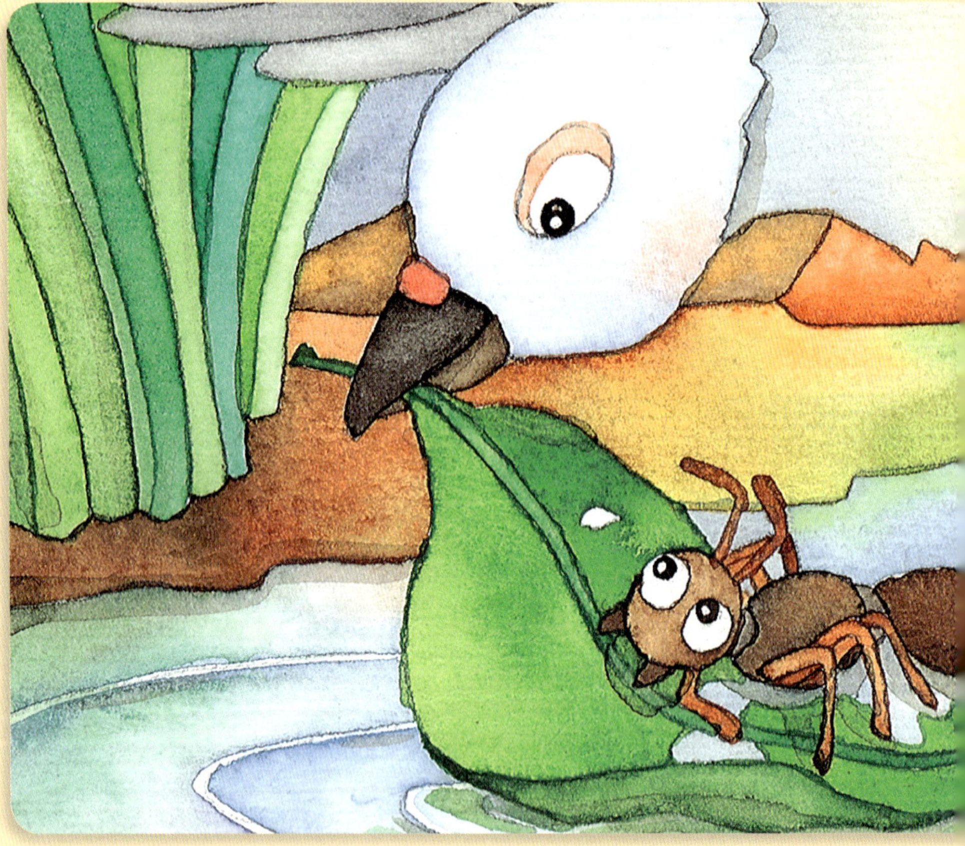

There once was a small red ant. He was taking a walk on a sunny morning and became very thirsty. He hurried ❶ to the river for a drink. However, he leaned over too far and fell into the water.

"Help!" he shouted. "I don't know how to swim! Somebody help me!"

A dove happened to fly by and saw the ant. She picked up a leaf ❷ and threw it into the water. The ant climbed onto the leaf and was safe.❸

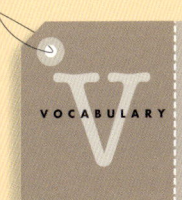

VOCABULARY

1. **hurry** v. ☞ 急ぐ
2. **leaf** n. ☞ 葉
3. **safe** adj. ☞ 安全な

"Thank you for saving me!" said the ant.

"You're welcome," answered the dove. "You are very small, so try to be more careful."❶

Later, the ant saw the dove sleeping in a tree. Under the tree, he saw a hunter with a net.❷ The ant crawled onto the hunter's foot and bit❸ him hard. The hunter yelled❹ and dropped his net. The dove woke up and flew away.

"Thank you," said the dove later. "You may be small, but your friendship is great and valuable."

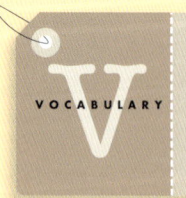

VOCABULARY

1. **careful** adj. ☞ 用心する
2. **net** n. ☞ 網
3. **bite** v. (bite-bit-bitten) ☞ 噛みつく
4. **yell** v. ☞ 叫ぶ

The Ant and the Dove **アリとハト** | 43

訳：アリとハト

　昔、小さくて赤いアリがいました。ある晴れた日の朝、散歩をしていると、とてものどが渇いてしまいました。アリは飲み水を求めて川に急ぎました。でも、身を乗り出しすぎて、水の中に落ちてしまったのです。
　「助けて!」　アリは叫びました。
「僕、泳げないんだ! 誰か助けて!」
　そこに一羽のハトが通りかかり、アリを見つけました。ハトは葉っぱをつまみ、川に投げました。ありは葉の上によじのぼり、助かりました。

　「助けてくれてありがとう!」　アリは言いました。
　「どういたしまして」　ハトは答えました。
「あなたはとても小さいんだから、もっと注意しないとね」
　後日、アリはハトが木で眠っているのを見かけました。木の下には、網をもったハンターがいます。アリは、ハンターの足の上を這って、強く咬みました。ハンターは叫び声を上げ、網を落としてしまいました。ハトは目を覚まし、飛び去りました。
　「ありがとう」
　あとで、ハトは言いました。
「あなたは小さいかもしれないけど、あなたの友情は偉大で素晴らしいわ」

【ことわざ】「情けは人の為ならず」

The Donkey and the Dog
ロバと
イヌ

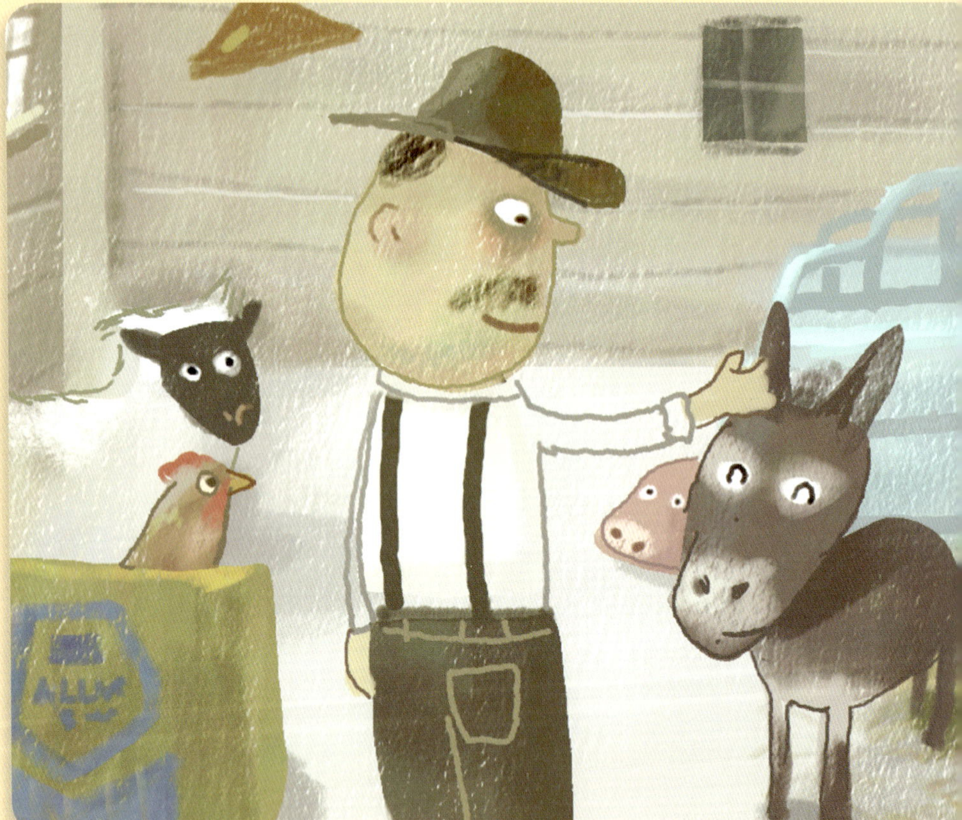

One day, a farmer went to see the animals in his stable.❶ His favorite donkey was there with other animals. The farmer often rode the donkey.

Because he was the farmer's favorite, the servants ❷ always fed him well and took care of him.

The farmer brought his dog with him that day. The dog was fat and clean. It danced and jumped happily and licked ❸ the farmer's hand.

The farmer took out some special food and gave it to the dog. When he sat to talk to his servants, the dog jumped onto his lap,❹ and there it sat gladly while the farmer scratched ❺ its ears.

VOCABULARY

1. **stable** n. ☞ 家畜小屋
2. **servant** n. ☞ 使用人
3. **lick** v. ☞ 〜をなめる
4. **lap** n. ☞ ひざ
5. **scratch** v. ☞ ひっかく

The Donkey and the Dog **ロバとイヌ**

The donkey saw the farmer give the dog some special food. He saw the farmer scratch its ears.

The farmer never treated ❶ the donkey so well.

The donkey broke loose and began dancing around the stable. He wanted to dance like the dog. He wanted to make the farmer like him, too.

But the farmer laughed and laughed until his stomach hurt. Then the donkey walked up to the farmer and tried to climb ❷ onto the farmer's lap, like the dog.

The servants quickly used sticks ❸ to hit the donkey to move him away. They quickly taught him a lesson: Do not try to be something that you are not.

VOCABULARY

1. **treat** v. ☞ 扱う
2. **climb** v. ☞ のぼる
3. **stick** n. ☞ 棒

The Donkey and the Dog **ロバとイヌ**

訳：ロバとイヌ

　ある日、農夫は小屋に動物たちの様子を見に行きました。お気に入りのロバは、ほかの動物たちと一緒にいました。農夫は、ときどきロバに乗りました。
　ロバは農夫のお気に入りだったので、使用人たちもロバにはいつも十分に食物を与え、よく面倒を見ていました。
　その日、農夫は、イヌを連れて来ました。イヌは丸々として清潔です。イヌはうれしそうに踊ったりジャンプをしたりして、農夫の手をなめました。
　農夫はごちそうを取り出し、イヌに与えました。農夫が使用人たちと話そうと座ると、イヌはそのひざの上に飛び乗り、農夫に耳をかいてもらいながら、そこに心地よさそうに座っていました。

　ロバは、農夫がイヌにごちそうを与えているのを見ました。そして、耳をかいてやっているのを見ました。
　農夫がロバに対してそんなふうにしてくれたことはありません。
　ロバは小屋を飛び出し、小屋の周りでダンスを踊り始めました。イヌと同じように踊りたかったのです。そして農夫に自分も気に入ってもらいたかったのです。
　でも、農夫はお腹が痛くなるまで笑いこけました。そしてロバは、農夫のもとに歩いていくと、イヌのように、農夫のひざの上によじ上ろうとしました。
　すぐに使用人たちは棒でロバを叩き、追いやりました。そしてすぐさま説教をしました。自分でないものになろうとしてはいけないのだ、と。

The City Mouse and the Country Mouse

都会のネズミと田舎のネズミ

The City Mouse and the Country Mouse **都会のネズミと田舎のネズミ** | 51

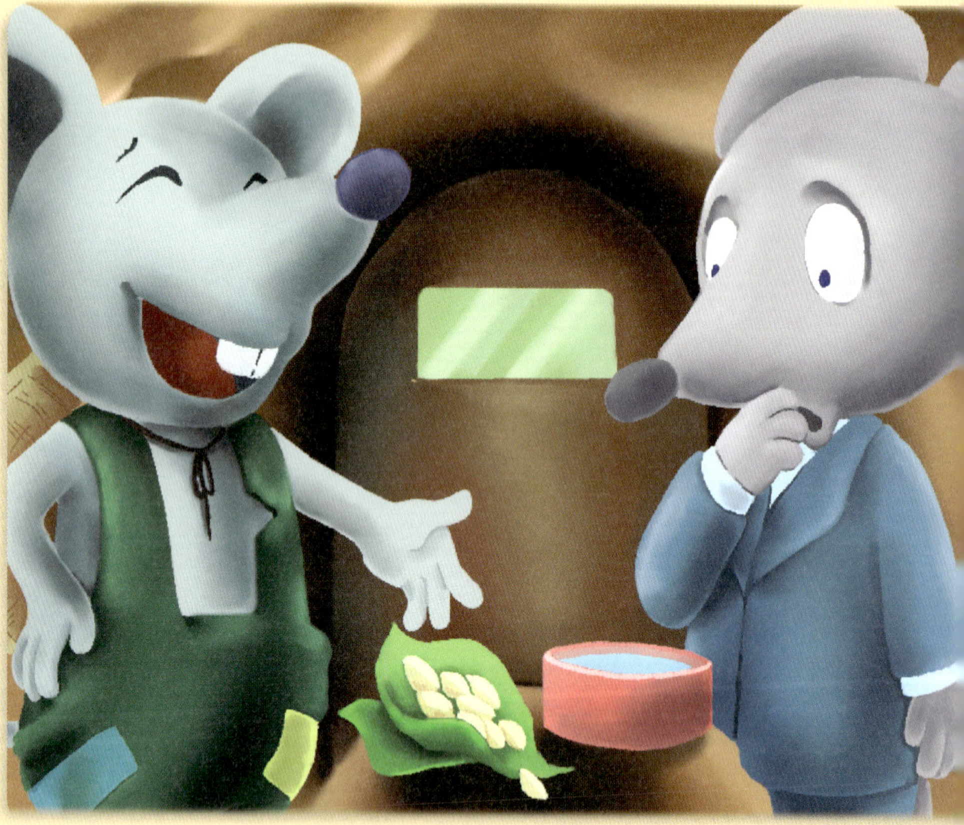

One day, a country mouse invited a city mouse to his house for dinner. The city mouse was happy. "I will eat a lot of wonderful[1] food!" he thought. But the country mouse only had some water and a little rice.

"You are very poor," said the city mouse. "Let's go to my house in the city. I have lots of delicious[2] food to eat."

The city mouse had cheese, cake, and honey.[3] He also had bread and lots of fruit. "You are so rich, and I am so poor," said the country mouse. "I wish I lived in the city, too!"

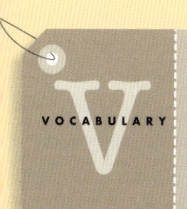

VOCABULARY

1. **wonderful** adj. ☞ すばらしい
2. **delicious** adj. ☞ おいしい
3. **honey** n. ☞ ハチミツ

Suddenly, they saw a cat. It had big teeth and sharp❶ claws,❷ and it tried to catch them. The country mouse and the city mouse ran into a hole and hid. They were frightened to death. The next time they tried to eat, a boy threw a shoe at them.

"Let's try again," said the city mouse. "It is a little dangerous,❸ but there is so much good food to eat!"

"No," said the country mouse, "I am going back to my house in the country. I only have rice to eat and water to drink, but I am safe and happy there."

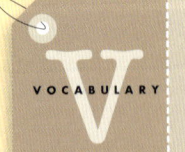

VOCABULARY

1. **sharp** adj. ☞ 鋭い
2. **claw** n. ☞ 爪
3. **dangerous** adj. ☞ あぶない

The City Mouse and the Country Mouse **都会のネズミと田舎のネズミ** | 55

訳：都会のネズミと田舎のネズミ

　ある日、田舎のネズミが都会のネズミを自宅へ食事に招きました。
　都会のネズミは喜び、
「おいしい食事をたくさん食べるぞ！」と思いました。
　でも、田舎のネズミが用意したのは水と少しの米だけでした。
　「君はとっても貧しいんだね」　都会のネズミは言いました。
「町にある僕の家に行こうよ。たくさんおいしい食べ物があるよ」
　都会のネズミの家には、チーズにケーキ、ハチミツ、そしてパンにたくさんのフルーツまでありました。
「君はとってもお金持ちなんだね。僕はすごく貧しいんだな」
　田舎のネズミは言いました。
「僕も都会に住んでいればなぁ！」

　そのとき突然、ネコが現れました。大きな歯と鋭い爪を持ったネコは、ネズミたちを捕まえようとします。田舎のネズミと都会のネズミは、穴の中に走り込んで隠れました。2匹は、死ぬほど怖い思いをしました。食べようとすると、今度は少年が2匹に向かって靴を投げてきました。
　「もう一度やってみよう」
　都会のネズミは言いました。
「ちょっと危険だけど、すっごくおいしいからね！」
　「いいや」
　田舎のネズミは言いました。
「僕は、田舎の家に帰るよ。食べ物は米、飲み物は水しかないけど、そこは安全だし、僕は幸せだから」

The Scorpion and the Frog
サソリとカエル

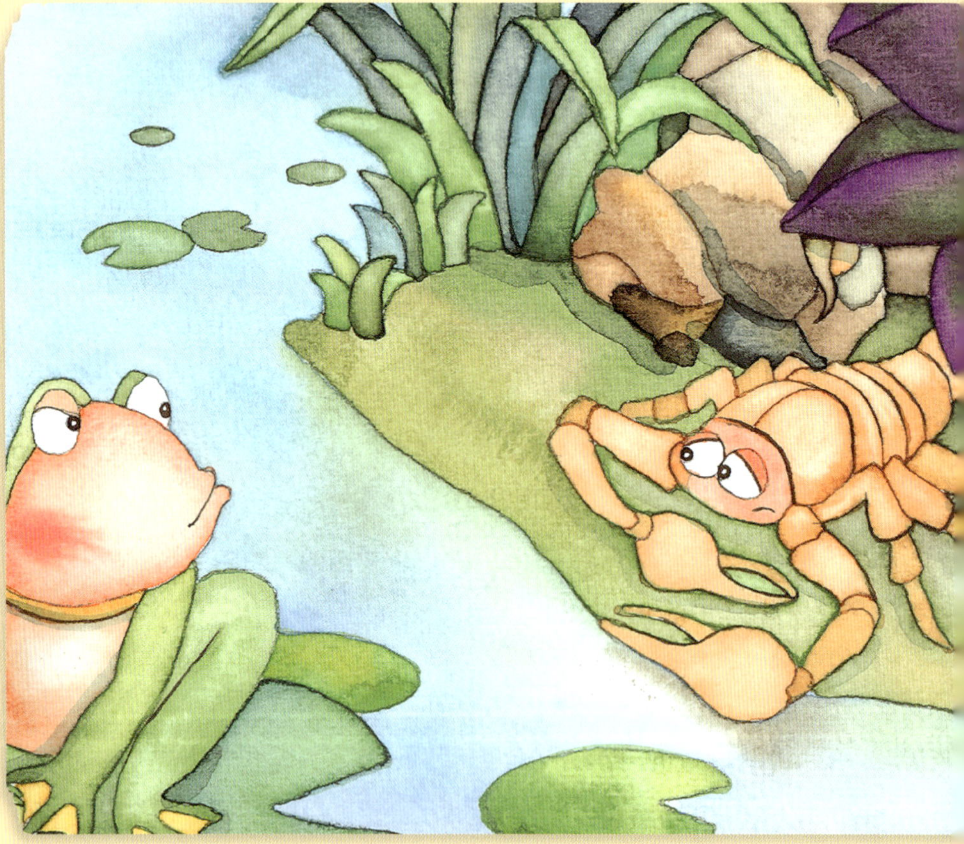

A scorpion ❶ and a frog met at the side of a river. The scorpion wanted to cross ❷ the river, but he didn't know how to swim.

"Please, Mr. Frog," he said, "would you carry ❸ me across the river?"

"I can't do that," said the frog. "You are a scorpion, and you will sting ❹ me."

"No," said the scorpion. "I won't sting you because then we will both drown in the river."

This made sense ❺ to the frog, and he agreed ❻ to help him.

VOCABULARY

1. **scorpion** n. ☞ サソリ
2. **cross** v. ☞ 渡る
3. **carry** v. ☞ 運ぶ
4. **sting** v. (sting-stung-stung) ☞ 刺す
5. **make sense** v. ☞ 筋が通っている
6. **agree** v. ☞ 合意する

The Scorpion and the Frog **サソリとカエル**

The scorpion climbed onto the back of the frog, and the frog began to swim. When they reached [1] the middle [2] of the river, the scorpion stung the frog. It hurt the frog very much, and they both began to sink under the water.

"Why did you sting me?" asked the frog. "Now I will die,[3] and you will surely drown."

"I couldn't help it," said the scorpion. "I am a scorpion, and that is what scorpions do. And you knew I was a scorpion when you let me ride [4] on your back."

VOCABULARY

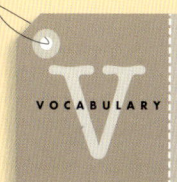

1. **reach** v. ☞ たどり着く
2. **middle** n. ☞ 真ん中
3. **die** v. ☞ 死ぬ
4. **ride** v. (ride-rode-ridden) ☞ 乗る

The Scorpion and the Frog **サソリとカエル**

訳：サソリとカエル

　サソリとカエルが川のほとりで出会いました。サソリは川を渡りたいのに、泳ぎ方がわかりません。
　「カエルさん、お願いです」
　サソリは言いました。
「僕を川の向こうに運んでくれませんか？」
　「できないよ」
　カエルは言います。
「君はサソリだもの。僕を刺すでしょ」
　「いいえ」
　サソリは答えます。
「刺しませんよ。だって、そうしたら僕もあなたも溺れてしまうもの」
　カエルは納得して、サソリを助けることにしました。

　サソリはカエルの背中によじ上り、カエルは泳ぎ始めました。川の中ごろにさしかかったとき、サソリはカエルを刺してしまいました。それはひどい痛みで、サソリもカエルも水の底に沈み始めました。
　「なんで僕を刺したんだよ！」
　カエルはたずねました。
「僕はもう死んじゃうし、君もきっとおぼれちゃうよ」
　「どうしようもなかったんですよ」
　サソリは言いました。
「だって僕はサソリだから。刺すからサソリなんです。あなたは、背中に僕を乗せてくれたとき、僕がサソリだってことを知っていたじゃないですか」

The Ant and the Grasshopper
アリとキリギリス

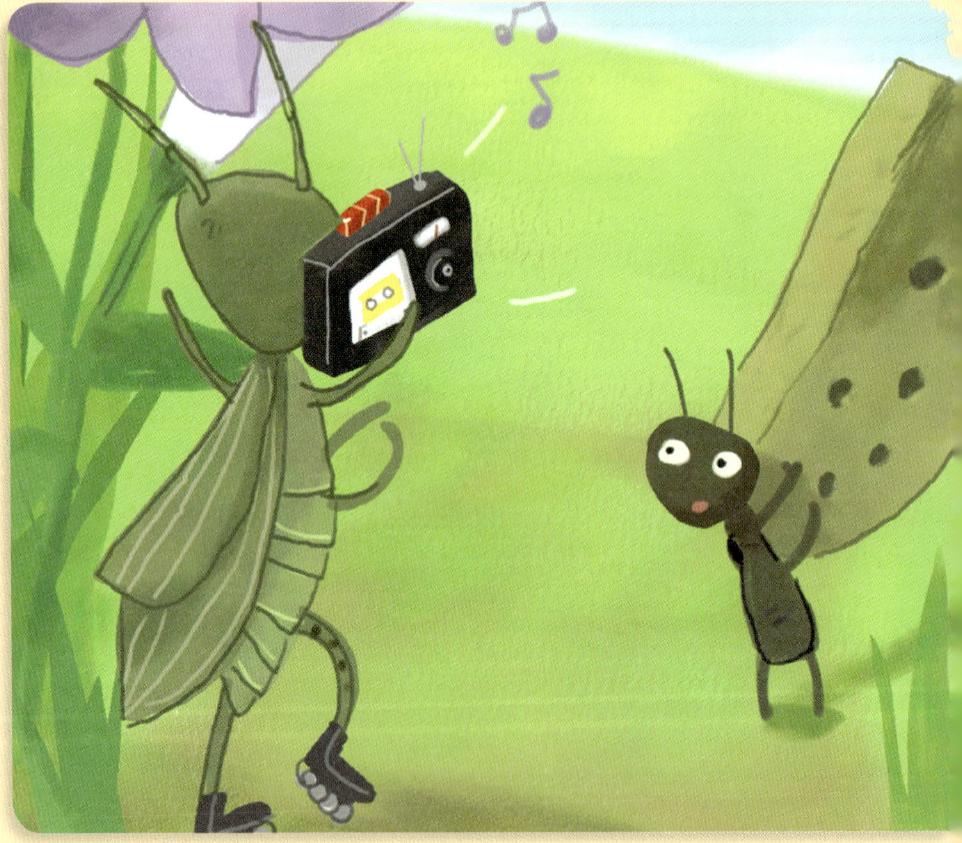

On a warm summer day, a grasshopper ❶ was dancing, singing, and fooling around.❷ He saw an ant pass by. The ant was carrying food on its back.

"Why don't you come and have fun with me?" asked the grasshopper. "Put down your heavy things and relax a little."

The ant stopped and said, "I am gathering ❸ food for the winter. I have much more to gather after this. I suggest ❹ that you gather food, too. Winter is coming."

The grasshopper laughed. "Why worry about winter? It's summer now. We have lots of food for summer. It is time to have fun!"

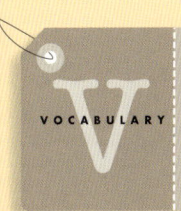

VOCABULARY

1. **grasshopper** n. ☞ キリギリス
2. **fool around** v. ☞ ダラダラ過ごす
3. **gather** v. ☞ 蓄える
4. **suggest** v. ☞ 勧める

Winter came, and it was a cold winter. It snowed every day and it was hard to find food.

The grasshopper grew hungry. The ant and his family, however, were happy. They ate the food that they had gathered during the summer. The ants passed by the grasshopper one windy day and noticed ❶ he was starving.❷

The grasshopper begged ❸ the ants for a little food. "Why didn't you gather food during the summer?" they asked.

"I was having too much fun," said the grasshopper.

And the ants said, "If you play all summer, you will be hungry all winter."

The grasshopper learned that you must work hard and prepare for the future.

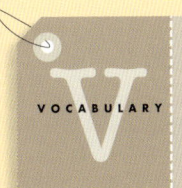

V VOCABULARY	1. **notice** v. ☞ 気づく
	2. **starve** v. ☞ おなかがペコペコである
	3. **beg** v. ☞ 懇願する

The Ant and the Grasshopper **アリとキリギリス** | 67

訳：アリとキリギリス

　ある暑い夏の日、キリギリスは、踊ったり歌ったり、ぶらぶら歩いたりして過ごしていました。そんなキリギリスは、一匹のアリが通り過ぎるのを見かけます。アリは背中に食物を載せて運んでいました。
「おいらと一緒に遊ばないかい?」 キリギリスはたずねました。
「重い荷物を下ろしてちょっとゆっくりしたらどう?」
　アリは立ち止まって言いました。
「冬に備えて食べ物を蓄えてるんだ。まだまだたくさん蓄えないと。君も蓄えておいたほうがいいよ。冬が来るから」
　キリギリスは笑いました。
「冬の心配だって? 今は夏だよ。夏にはたくさん食べ物がある。今は楽しむときなんだよ!」

　冬が来ました。寒い冬でした。毎日雪が降り、食べ物を見つけるのは至難の業。
　キリギリスはだんだんお腹が減ってきました。でも、あのアリとその家族は幸せでした。夏の間に蓄えておいた食べ物を食べていたからです。ある風の強い日、キリギリスのそばを通り過ぎたアリたちは、キリギリスがお腹を空かしていることに気付きました。
　キリギリスは、アリに少し食べ物をくれないかと乞いました。
　「なんで君は夏の間に食べ物を蓄えておかなかったの?」
　アリたちはたずねました。
　「楽しいことがたくさんあったから」とキリギリスは言いました。
　するとアリたちは言いました。
「夏の間中遊んでいたら、冬の間中、お腹をすかせていることになるんだよ」
キリギリスは、一生懸命働いて未来に備えないといけないことを学んだのです。

The Dancing Monkeys
踊るおサルさん

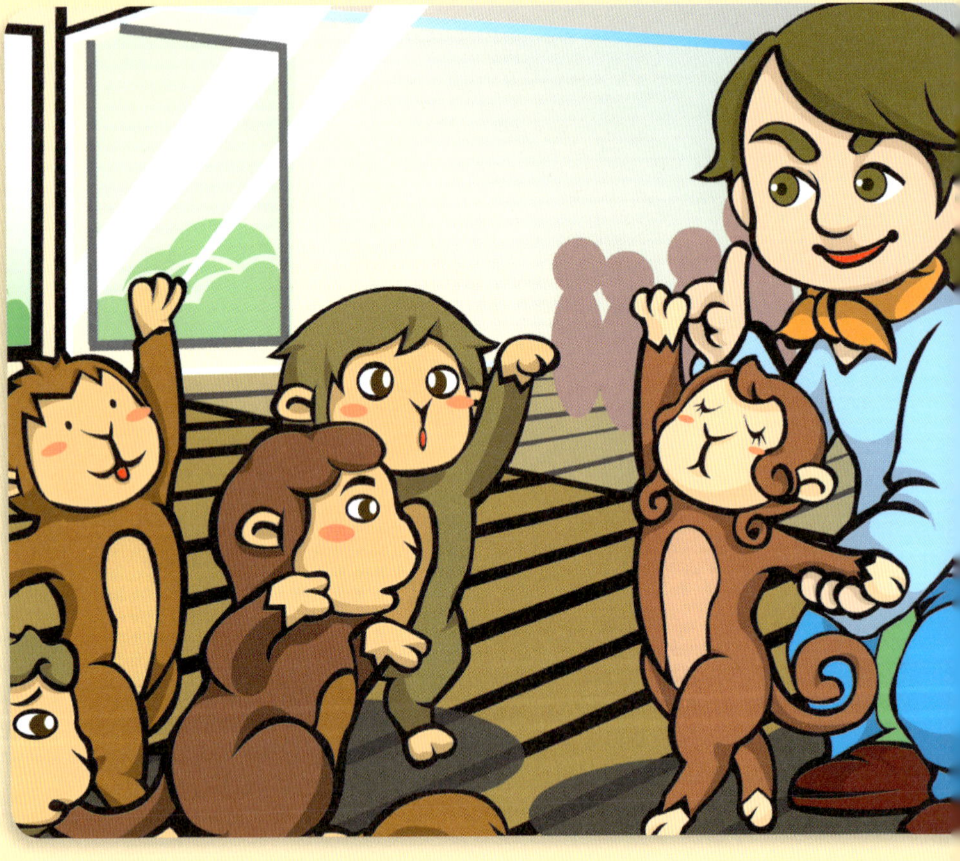

Once upon a time, a man taught some monkeys how to dance. The monkeys were very clever,[1] and they learned how to dance very well.

The man was very happy. He dressed the monkeys up in fancy[2] clothes and masks. Then he took them to a party. He wanted people to admire[3] his dancing monkeys.

The dancing monkeys were very popular at the party. Nobody knew they were monkeys, and everyone enjoyed watching them dance.

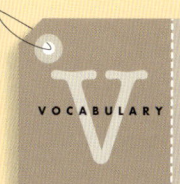

VOCABULARY

1. **clever** adj. ☞ 賢い
2. **fancy** adj. ☞ 派手な
3. **admire** v. ☞ 賞賛する

Then a naughty ❶boy threw some bananas in front of the dancing monkeys. At the sight of ❷ the bananas, the monkeys forgot all about dancing. They tore ❸off their masks and rushed over to the bananas and began to eat.

All the people at the party began to laugh. "They aren't dancers at all," said one guest. "They're just monkeys! I guess not everything you see is what it appears to be!"

"And," said another, "You should never try to be something you're not."

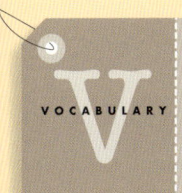

V VOCABULARY	1. **naughty** adj. ☞ いたずら好きな 2. **at the sight of~** ☞ ～を見て 3. **tear** v. (tear-tore-torn) ☞ むしり取る

訳：踊るおサルさん

　昔々、一人の男がサルたちにダンスを教えました。サルたちはとても賢く、すぐにダンスを覚えました。
　男はとても満足し、サルたちをきれいな衣装とお面で着飾らせ、パーティーに連れていきました。男は人間たちに、踊るサルたちを自慢したかったのです。
　踊るサルたちはパーティーの人気者になりました。誰も彼らがサルであることに気付かず、誰もがそのダンスを楽しみました。

　そのとき、いたずらっ子の少年が、踊るサルたちの前にバナナを投げました。バナナを見たサルたちはダンスのことなどすっかり忘れ、お面をむしり取ってバナナに向かって突進、食べ始めました。
　パーティーに来ていた人々は笑い始めました。
「ダンサーなんかじゃない」
　一人のお客が言いました。
「ただのサルだよ。見えるものすべてが、外見通りとは限らない、ということだね」
　「それから」
　と別のお客が言いました。
「自分でないものになろうとしてはいけない、ということさ」

【ことわざ】「人は見かけによらぬもの」
　　　　　　「鵜のまねをする烏」

The Farmer's Daughter
農夫の娘

A farmer's ❶daughter was walking to the market with a bucket of milk on her head. As she walked, she started to make plans.

"I will get some money for this milk. With that money, I will buy fifty eggs," she said. "In a couple of weeks, those eggs will hatch,❷ and I will have fifty chickens."

"I will give those chickens good food, and they will grow ❸big and fat. Then I will take them to the market and sell them. I will make lots of money!"

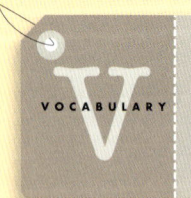

VOCABULARY

1. **farmer** n. ☞ 農夫
2. **hatch** v. ☞ (卵が) かえる
3. **grow** v. (grow-grew-grown) ☞ 育つ

The Farmer's Daughter **農夫の娘** | 77

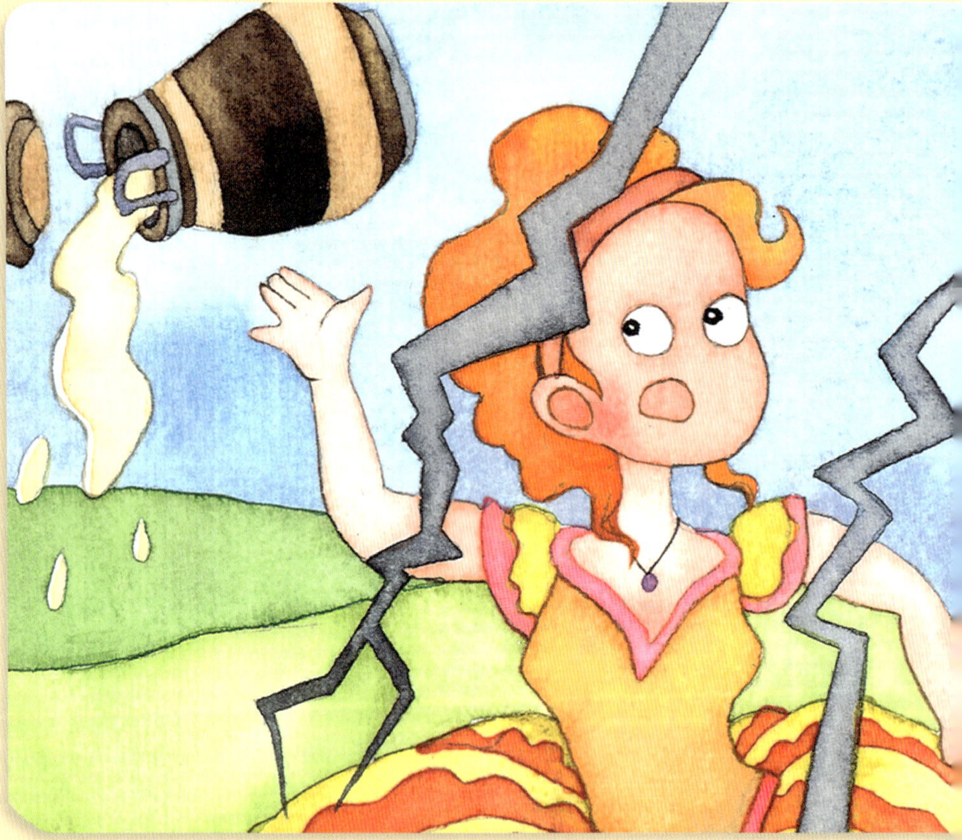

"I'll take that money and buy a beautiful dress," she said. "I will go to parties, and all the boys will want to dance with me. The other girls will be jealous, but I don't care. I'll toss my head,[1] like this."

As she spoke, she tossed her head. The bucket fell[2] off her head, and all the milk spilled[3] on the ground. She had to go home and tell her mother what happened.

"Ah, child," said her mother, "you shouldn't count your chickens before they hatch."

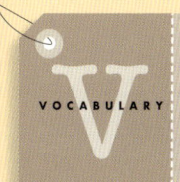

VOCABULARY

1. **toss one's head** v. ☞ 頭をぷいっと上げる
2. **fall** v. (fall-fell-fallen) ☞ 落ちる
3. **spill** v. ☞ こぼす

訳：農夫の娘

　農夫の娘が手桶一杯のミルクを頭に載せて市場に向かって歩いていました。歩きながら、娘は計画を練り始めました。
「このミルクでいくらかお金が入るから、そのお金で 50 個の卵を買いましょう」
　娘は言います。
「2 ～ 3 週間もすれば、卵がかえって、50 羽のニワトリになるわ」
　「ニワトリに栄養のある食事を与えれば、丸々と大きく育つでしょう。そうしたら市場に持って行って売るの。お金がたくさん入るわ！」

　「そのお金できれいなドレスを買いましょう」
　と娘は言いました。
「パーティーに行けば、男の子たちはみんな私とダンスを踊りたがるわ。ほかの女の子たちは嫉妬するでしょうけど、気にしない。私は、頭を上げるの。こんなふうにね」
　話しながら、娘は頭をくいっと上げました。すると手桶は頭から落ち、ミルクはすべて地面にこぼれてしまいました。娘は家に帰って、母親に事の次第を話さなくてはいけませんでした。
　「まぁ、この子ったら」　母親は言いました。
「卵がかえる前に、ニワトリの数を数えてはいけないのよ」

　　　　　　　　　　　　　　　　　　【ことわざ】「取らぬ狸の皮算用」

The Man, the Boy, and the Donkey

男と少年とロバ

One day, a man and his son were walking with their donkey [1] to a market. As they walked, a man passed by. He said, "You fools! Why don't you ride the donkey?"

So the man told his son to get on the donkey, and they walked on.

Soon, they saw some other men. One said, "What a lazy [2] boy! He rides and his father walks!"

So the man told the boy to get off, and he got on himself.

Soon, they saw some women. One woman said, "Shame on you! [3] You ride and your son walks!"

The man felt ashamed. [4]

VOCABULARY

1. **donkey** n. ☞ ロバ
2. **lazy** adj. ☞ 怠惰な
3. **shame on you!** ☞ 恥を知れ!
4. **ashamed** adj. ☞ 恥ずかしい

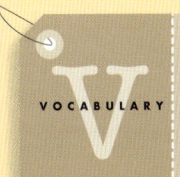

The Man, the Boy, and the Donkey **男と少年とロバ** | 83

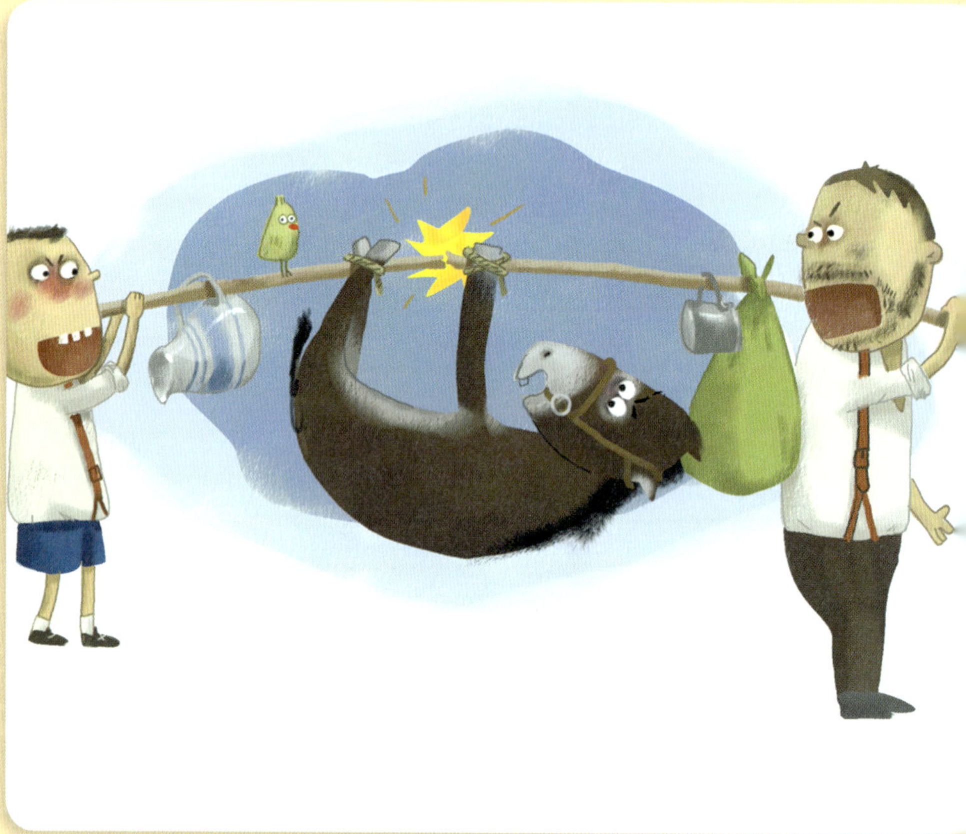

So the man put the boy on the donkey with him and they walked on. As they got close to the market, people began to look at them. People asked, "Why are you overloading[1] your donkey?"

Now, the man and the boy thought and thought. Then they took a pole[2] and tied the donkey's legs to it. They put the pole on their shoulders and carried the donkey between them.

People laughed and laughed, and when they crossed a bridge,[3] the pole broke and the donkey fell into the river.

An old man laughed and said, "If you try to please everyone, you will not please anyone."

VOCABULARY

1. **overload** v. ☞ 荷を積みすぎている
2. **pole** n. ☞ 棒
3. **bridge** n. ☞ 橋

The Man, the Boy, and the Donkey

訳：男と少年とロバ

　ある日、一人の男と少年がロバと一緒に市場へと歩いていました。
　道の途中、一人の男が通りすがりに言いました。
「バカだな。なんでロバに乗らないんだ」
　そこで、男は息子にロバに乗るように言い、彼らはまた歩きました。
　間もなく、別の男に会いました。その男は言います。
「なんて怠け者の坊主なんだ。自分はロバに乗って、父親を歩かせているなんて」
　そこで、男は息子に、ロバから降りるように言い、今度は自分が乗りました。
　間もなく、女たちに会いました。一人の女が言いました。
「なんてことでしょう。自分はロバに乗って、息子を歩かせているなんて」
　男は恥ずかしくなりました。

　そこで男は息子と一緒にロバに乗り、また歩き始めました。
　市場が近くなってくると、人々がじろじろ見始めました。人々は聞きました。
「なんで、自分のロバにそんなにたくさん背負わせているんだ」
　さて、男と少年は考えに考えました。そして二人は棒を持ってくると、ロバの足を縛り付けました。棒を担ぐと、ロバを間にして運びました。
　人々は大笑いしています。そして、彼らが橋を渡っていると、棒が折れてロバは川に落ちてしまいました。
　一人の老人は笑って言いました。
「すべての人を満足させようとすると、誰も満足させられないということだよ」

The Lioness
めすライオン

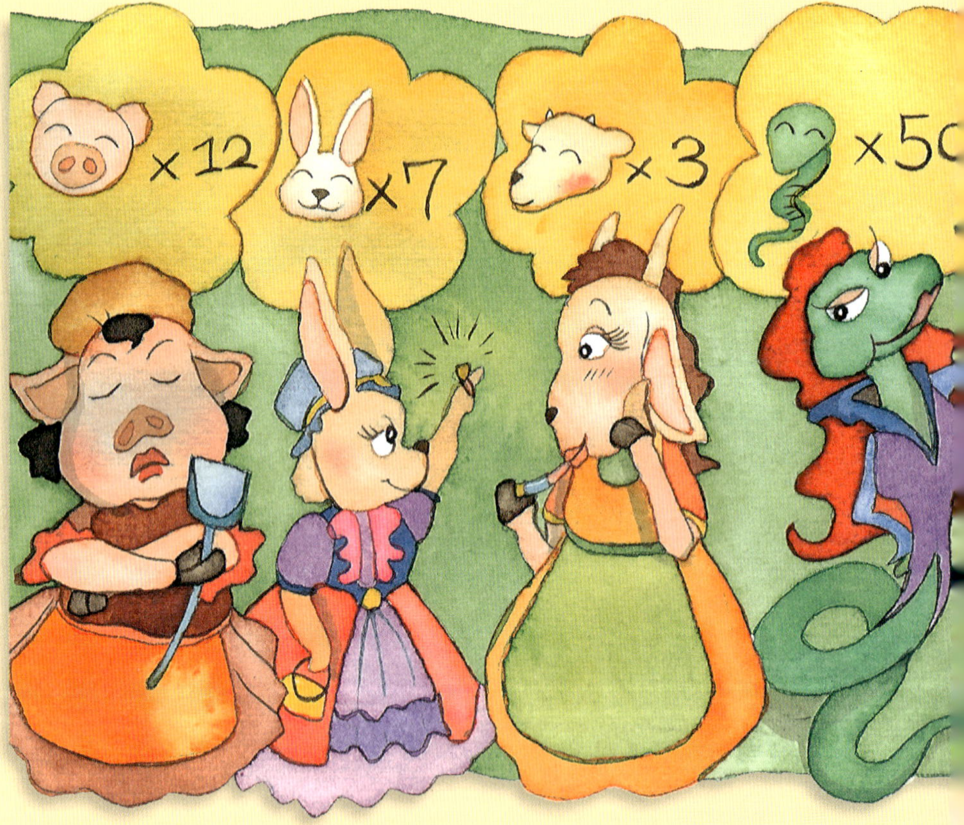
×12
×7
×3

One day, some animals were talking about which animal was the best. The pig said, "Pigs are the greatest because we have many babies. I have twelve healthy[1] little pigs." She asked the rabbit, "How many babies do you have?"

The rabbit felt embarrassed.[2] She only had seven. Then she pointed at the sheep and said, "She only has three!" Everyone laughed.

A snake passed by[3] and said, "Snakes are truly[4] the greatest. I have fifty!"

"So what?" said a new voice. Everyone turned around[5] and saw a lioness.[6]

VOCABULARY

1. **healthy** adj. ☞ 健康な
2. **embarrassed** adj. ☞ 恥ずかしい
3. **pass by** v. ☞ 〜のそばを通る
4. **truly** adv. ☞ 本当に
5. **turn around** v. ☞ 振り向く
6. **lioness** n. ☞ 雌ライオン

The snake lifted up her head and looked at the lioness. "Why do you speak? I have fifty babies. You only have one. That's nothing." The other animals said that the snake was right.

The lioness laughed. "I only have one, but it is a lion. Only a lion can be the king of the forest."

The other animals could think of nothing to say. They had many babies, but none of them would ever be as strong as a lion. "One valuable ❶ thing," said the lioness, "is worth ❷ more than a hundred common ❸ ones."

VOCABULARY

1. **valuable** adj. ☞ 貴重な
2. **worth** adj. ☞ 価値がある
3. **common** adj. ☞ ありふれた、普通の

The Lioness **めすライオン** | 91

The Lioness

訳：めすライオン

　ある日、動物たちは、どの動物が最上の動物かを話し合っていました。ブタは言いました。
「ブタは子だくさんだからいちばん偉大よ。私には12匹の健康な小さなブタがいるわ」
ブタはウサギに聞きました。
「あなたの子供は何匹？」
　ウサギは困ってしまいました。7匹の子供しかいなかったからです。そしてウサギはヒツジを指差して言いました。
「ヒツジさんはたったの3匹よ！」
みんなが笑いました。
　1匹のヘビが通りかかり、言いました。
「本当に偉いのはヘビ。私には50匹いるわ！」
　「だから何？」
別の声がしました。みんなが振り返ると、めすライオンがいました。

ヘビは頭をもたげ、めすライオンを見ました。
「なんで、そう言うの？　私には50匹の赤ちゃんがいるわ。あなたは1頭だけでしょ。話にならない」
ほかの動物たちもヘビが正しいと言いました。
　めすライオンは笑いました。
「1頭だけだけど、ライオンよ。ライオンだけが森の王になれるの」
　ほかの動物たちは言うべきことを思いつくことができませんでした。動物たちにはたくさんの赤ちゃんがいましたが、どれもライオンほど強くはなれないのです。めすライオンは言いました。
「貴重なものは、たとえひとつでも普通のもの100以上の価値があるのよ」

The Farmer and the Goats
農夫とヤギ

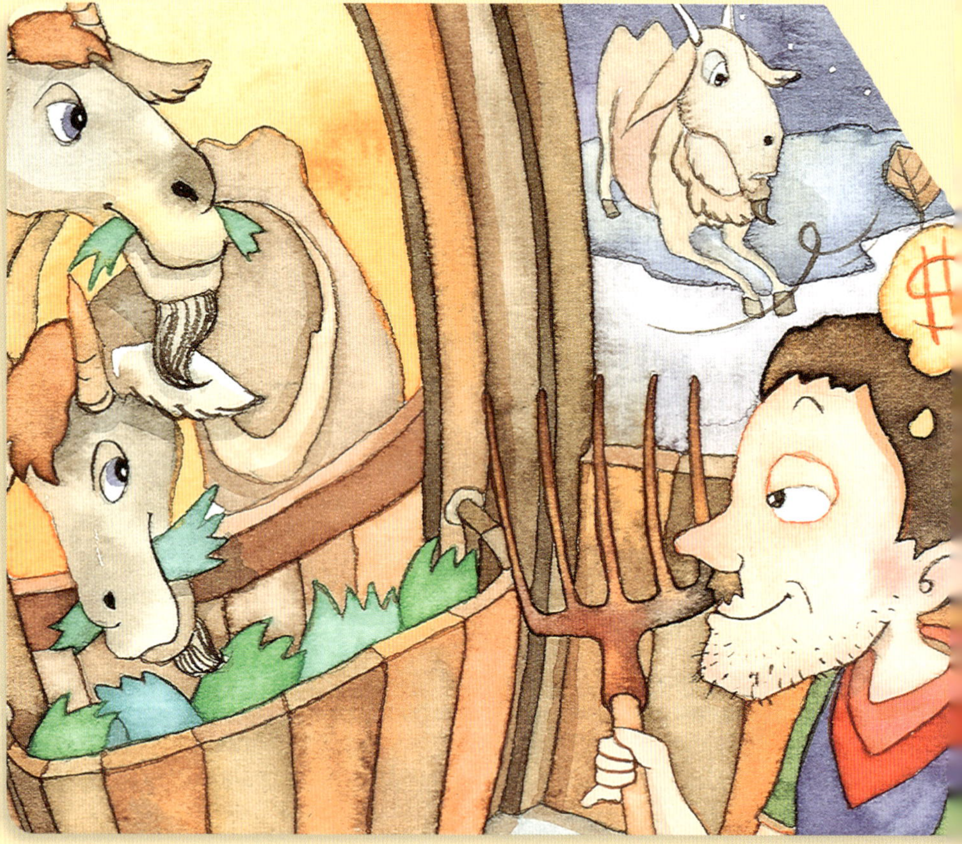

One stormy winter night, a farmer noted **❶** that another farmer's goats were on his land. He was quite excited. "If these new goats stay here, I could sell them in the spring," he thought.

The farmer made sure that the new goats were comfortable.**❷** He let them stay in the warm barn and gave them large piles of hay to eat.

Meanwhile, he showed no concern **❸** for his old goats. He left them out in the bitter **❹** wind and gave them almost no food. They were cold and hungry all night long.

VOCABULARY

1. **note** v. ☞ 〜に気付く
2. **comfortable** adj. ☞ 快適な
3. **concern** n. ☞ 気遣い
4. **bitter** adj. ☞ 厳しい

The next morning, the storm was over and the sun was shining.❶ When the farmer opened the barn doors, the goats rushed out as quickly as they could. "How can you leave?" shouted the farmer angrily. "I was so generous❷ to all of you!"

"Yes," said one of the goats, "but you ignored your own goats on a stormy night. We fear❸ that one day, you would be careless❹ with us, too."

The farmer learned that you shouldn't forget about old friends when you are trying to make new ones.

VOCABULARY

1. **shine** v. (shine-shone-shone) ☞ 輝く
2. **generous** adj. ☞ 寛大な
3. **fear** v. ☞ 不安
4. **careless** adj. ☞ ぞんざいな

The Farmer and the Goats 農夫と**ヤギ**

訳：農夫とヤギ

　ある嵐の冬の夜、農夫は、別の農夫のヤギが自分の敷地にいることに気付きました。農夫はたいそう興奮しました。
「新しいヤギたちがここにとどまれば、春にヤツらを売れるぞ」
　そう思ったからです。
　農夫は、新しいヤギたちが居心地よさそうにしているのを確かめました。暖かい納屋に入れ、干し草をたっぷり与えました。
　この間、農夫は古くからいるヤギたちを気にかけませんでした。寒風の中に置き去りにし、食事もほとんど与えなかったのです。ヤギたちは一晩中、寒さと飢えの中で過ごしました。

　翌朝、嵐は過ぎ去り、太陽が輝いています。農夫が納屋を開けると、ヤギたちは全速力で走り去ってしまいました。
「よくも出ていけるもんだな！」
　農夫は怒って叫びました。
「お前たち全員に親切にしてやったじゃないか」
　「そうだよ」
　一匹のヤギが言いました。
「でも君は嵐の夜、自分のヤギたちを放置した。僕たちも、いつか見放されるんじゃないかって心配になったのさ」
　農夫は学んだのです。新しい友だちを作ろうとするときも、古くからの友人を忘れてはいけないということを。

The Boy Who Cried Wolf
オオカミ少年

100

There once was a boy who watched his family's sheep each day. One day, he was bored ❶ and wanted to have some fun.

He shouted ❷ to the people in the town,❸ "Wolf! Wolf! A wolf is trying to eat my sheep!"

Many people from the town ran to him. When they got there, there was no wolf. There was only the boy, and he was laughing at them because they ran there for nothing.

Another day, the boy was bored, and again he shouted, "Wolf! Wolf!" People from the town ran to him, but the boy just laughed at them again.

VOCABULARY

1. **bored** adj. ☞ 退屈した
2. **shout** v. ☞ 大声を出す
3. **town** n. ☞ 町

The Boy Who Cried Wolf **オオカミ少年**

Then, one day, a wolf really did attack ❶ the boy's sheep. The boy shouted, "Wolf! Wolf! A wolf is attacking my sheep! Help! Help!" He was very afraid and he shouted again and again.

But the people in town who heard him thought, "The boy is only trying to play a trick on us." And no one went to help him.

The wolf killed all of the boy's sheep.

This is a very old and well-known ❷ fable. ❸ It has an important lesson: If you often lie, people will not believe you, even when you tell the truth.

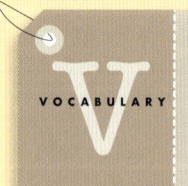

VOCABULARY

1. **attack** v. ☞ ～を襲う
2. **well-known** adj. ☞ よく知られた
3. **fable** n. ☞ 寓話

The Boy Who Cried Wolf **オオカミ少年** | 103

訳：オオカミ少年

　昔々、毎日、家族のヒツジの番をしている少年がいました。ある日、見張りに飽きてしまった少年は面白いことがしたくなります。
　少年は、町の人たちに向かって叫びました。
「オオカミだ！ オオカミだ！ オオカミが僕のヒツジを食べようとしているよ！」
　町から人が大勢走ってきました。現場に着くと、オオカミはいません。いるのは少年だけです。少年は、なんの役にも立たないのに走ってきた人々を見て笑っていました。
　その後のある日、少年は退屈して、また叫びました。
「オオカミだ！ オオカミだ！」　町の人々は少年のもとに走って来ました。でも、少年はまたもや、そんな彼らを笑うだけです。

　そしてある日、一匹のオオカミが本当に少年のヒツジを襲ったのです。
　少年は叫びました。
「オオカミだ！ オオカミだ！ オオカミが僕のヒツジを襲っているよー！助けて！ 助けて！」
　少年はとても怖くて、何度も何度も叫びました。
　でも、叫び声を聞いた町の人はこう思いました。
「あの少年は、わしらを一杯食わそうとしてるだけさ」
　そして、誰も少年を助けには行きませんでした。
　オオカミは、少年のヒツジを全部食べてしまいました。
　これは、とても古くから伝わる物語ですが、この物語には大事な教訓があります。それは、うそばかりついていると、たとえ本当のことを言っていても人は信用してくれなくなる、ということです。

The Wizard and the Gold Umbrella
魔法使いと金の傘

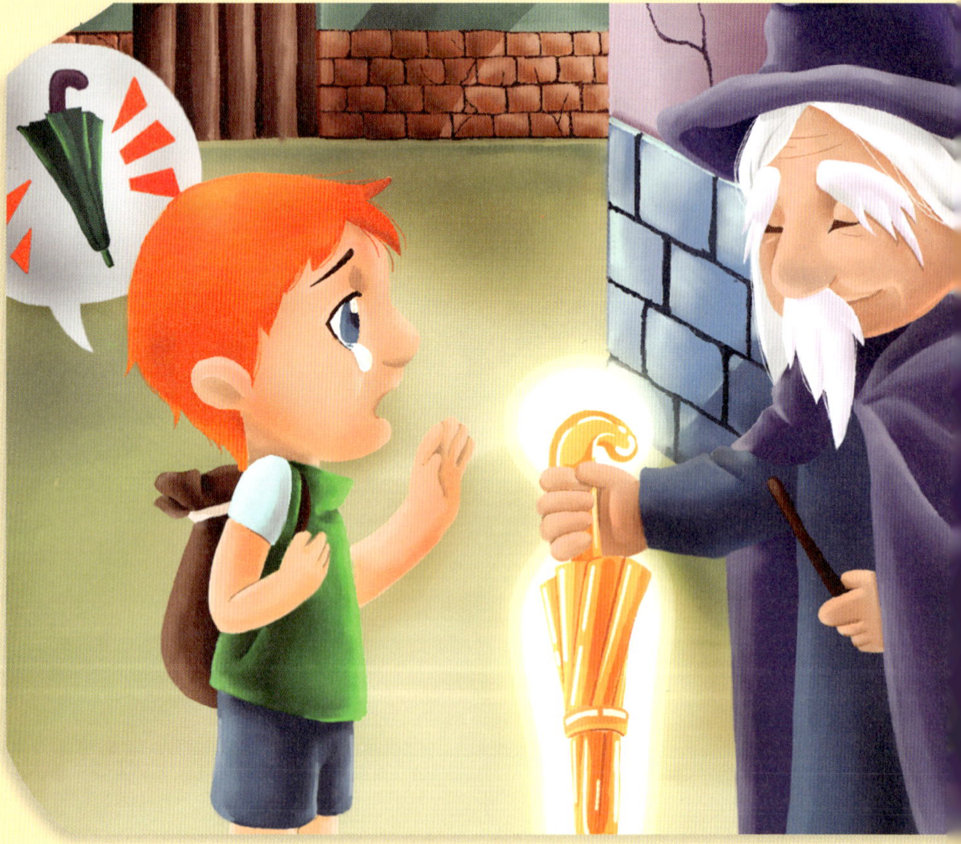

One day, a boy lost his umbrella. He was very sad. "It is going to rain and I am going to get wet!" he cried.

A wizard ❶ heard the boy and showed him a gold umbrella. "Is this your umbrella?" he asked. The boy was very honest ❷ and said, "No, my umbrella was not made of gold."

Then the wizard showed him a silver umbrella. "That isn't my umbrella, either," said the boy.

Finally, the wizard showed him his original ❸ umbrella. "That's my umbrella!" said the boy.

The wizard said, "You are an honest boy and I will give you all three umbrellas!"

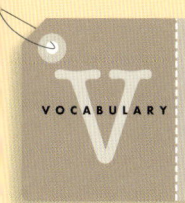

VOCABULARY

1. **wizard** n. ☞ 魔法使い
2. **honest** adj. ☞ 正直な
3. **original** adj. ☞ 元の

A greedy ❶ stranger ❷ heard this story and had an idea. He went to the wizard and said, "I lost my umbrella, too!"

The wizard showed him a beautiful gold umbrella. "Is this your umbrella?" he asked.

The greedy stranger smiled. "Yes, that is my umbrella," he lied. "Give it to me!"

Instead of giving him the umbrella, the wizard clapped ❷ his hands once, and it began to rain. Soon the greedy man was wet and cold.

The wizard said, "An honest man gets more than he loses. A dishonest man gets nothing. I will not give you any umbrellas."

VOCABULARY

1. **greedy** adj. ☞ 欲張りな
2. **stranger** n. ☞ 見知らぬ人
3. **clap** v. ☞ (手を) たたく

訳：魔法使いと金の傘

ある日、一人の少年が傘をなくしてしまいました。少年はとても悲しくなりました。
「雨が降り出しそうだ。僕、濡れちゃうよ」 そう言って泣きました。
　魔法使いは、少年の声を聞き、金の傘を見せて聞きました。
「これは君の傘かな？」 とても正直な少年は言いました。
「違います。僕の傘は金ではできていません」
　すると、魔法使いは銀の傘を見せました。
「これも僕の傘ではありません」 少年は言いました。
　最後に、魔法使いは少年の傘を見せました。
「これが僕の傘です！」 少年は言いました。
　魔法使いは言いました。
「君は正直者だな。3本の傘をすべて君にあげよう」

　欲張りな人間がこの話を聞き、ある計画を思いつきました。彼は魔法使いのところに行き、言ったのです。
「僕も傘をなくしてしまいました！」
　魔法使いは美しい金の傘を見せて聞きました。
「これが君の傘かな？」
　欲深い人間は微笑みました。
「そうです。僕の傘です」 彼はウソをついたのです。
「それを僕にください」
　魔法使いは、彼に傘を与えるかわりに、一回手をたたきました。すると雨が降り出し、欲張り男はすぐに濡れて冷えてしまいました。
　魔法使いは言いました。
「正直者は、なくした物より多くを得る。嘘つきは何も得られない。お前にはどんな傘もやらないよ」

The King and His Two Wives
王様と2人のお妃

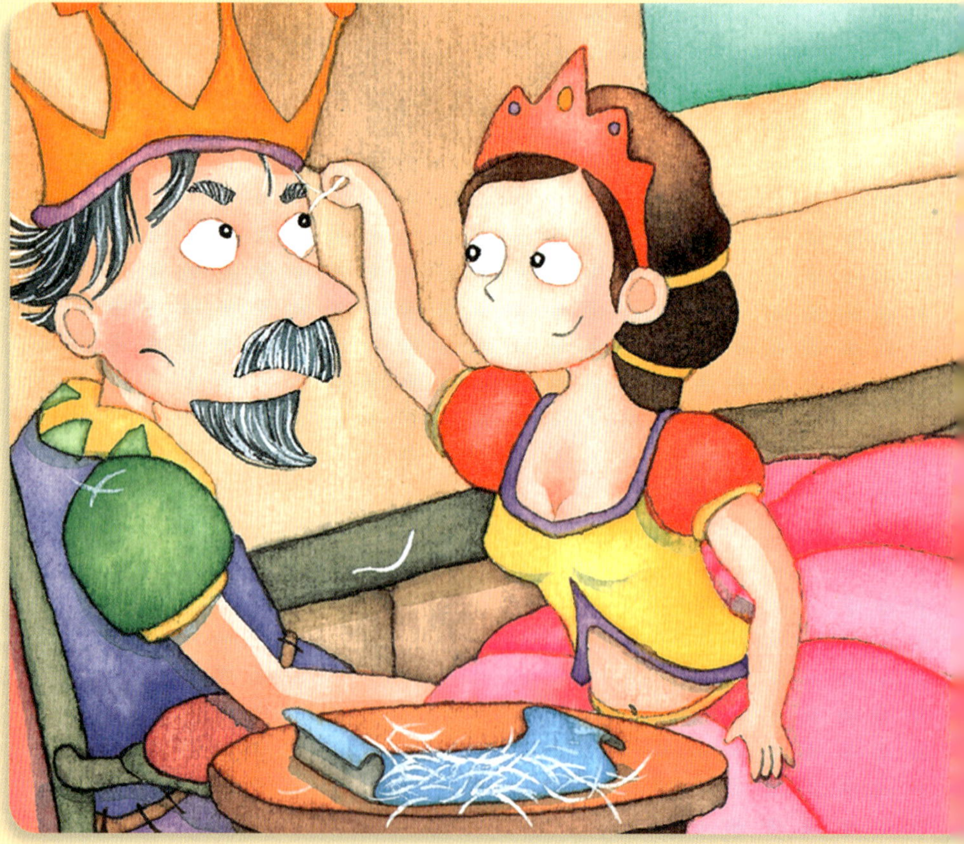

Once upon a time, there was a king[1] who had two wives.[2] One was younger than the king, and the other was older. Both wives loved the king, but the young wife was unhappy[3] because the king's hair was starting to turn gray.[4]

"I don't want a husband who looks so old," said the young wife. "People will think I'm his daughter!" So each night, she pulled out some of his gray hair.

"Ouch!" said the king. But he wanted his young wife to be happy, and he didn't stop her.

VOCABULARY

1. **king** n. ☞ 王
2. **wife** n. ☞ 妻
3. **unhappy** adj. ☞ 不幸せな
4. **gray** adj. ☞ 白髪の

The King and His Two Wives 王様と2人のお妃

The older wife was happy that the king's hair was turning gray. "Now people will stop thinking I'm his mother," she said. And each morning, she pulled out some of the king's black hair.

"Ouch!" said the king. But he wanted his older wife to be happy, and he didn't stop her, either.

Soon, the king had no hair left at all. Both of his wives cried[1] when they saw how silly[2] he looked. "Oh, well," said the king. "If you try to please[3] everyone, you end up pleasing no one."

VOCABULARY

1. **cry** v. ☞ 泣く
2. **silly** adj. ☞ 間抜けな
3. **please** v. ☞ 〜を喜ばせる

The King and His Two Wives **王様と2人のお妃** | 115

訳：王様と2人のお妃

　昔々、2人のお妃をもつ王様がいました。お妃の1人は王様より年下で、もう1人は年上でした。2人とも王様を愛していましたが、若いお妃は、王様の髪の毛が白髪になり始めたので、悲しんでいました。
　「年寄りくさく見えるだんな様はいやです」
　若いお妃は言いました。
「人は私を娘だと思うことでしょう！」
　お妃は、毎晩、王様の白髪を抜きました。
　「イタタ！」
　王様は言います。でも、若いお妃を幸せにしたかった王様は、止めませんでした。

　年上のお妃は、王様の髪が白髪になってきたことをうれしく思っていました。
　「これで、私が王様の母親だと思う人はいなくなるでしょう」
　とお妃は言います。そして毎朝、王様の黒い髪の毛を抜きました。
　「イタタ！」
　王様は言います。でも、年上のお妃を幸せにしたかった王様は、こちらも止めませんでした。
　やがて王様はつるっぱげになってしまいました。2人のお妃は、王様の間抜けな姿を見て嘆きました。
「う〜む」
　王様は言いました。
「みんなを喜ばせようとすると、誰も喜ばない結果になってしまうんだな」

The Lion and the Mouse
ライオンとネズミ

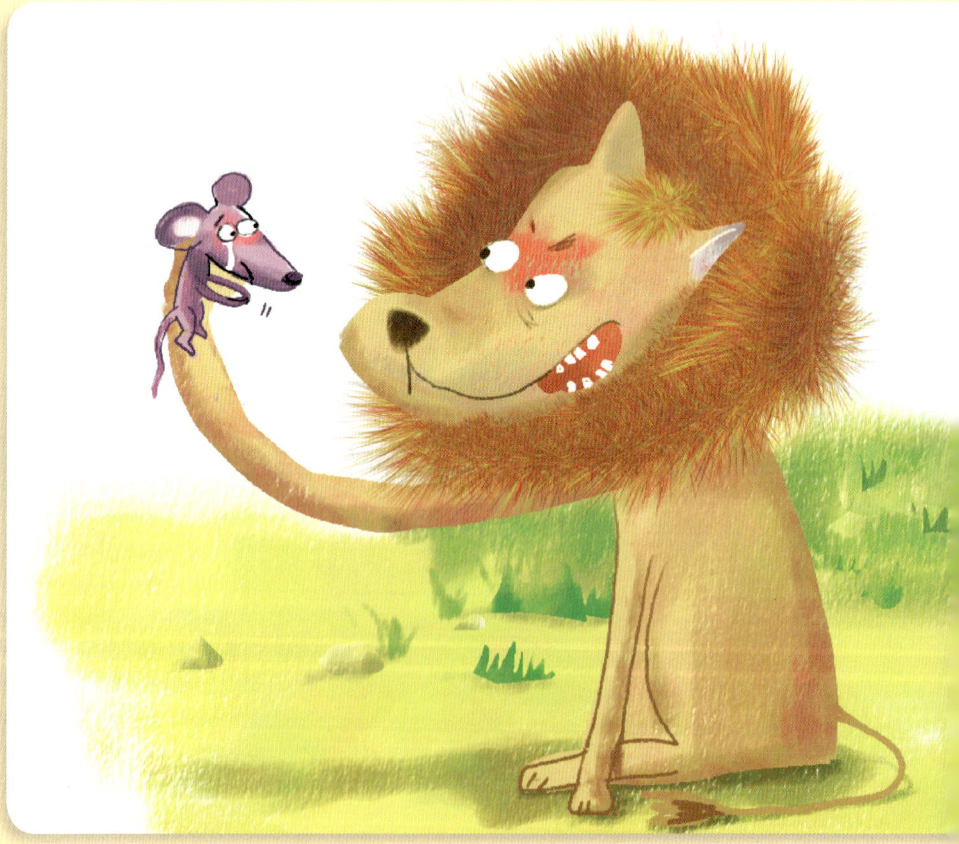

One day, a mouse accidentally bumped into① a sleeping lion's paw.② The lion woke up and put his great big paw over the mouse.

The mouse said, "I'm sorry! Don't hurt me!"

The lion picked up the mouse to eat him.

"Please forgive③ me!" the mouse cried. "I won't forget it. I might be able to help you one day."

The lion laughed at this. "How can a little mouse help a big lion?" he asked. "But you have made me laugh, so I will let you go."

He put the mouse down, and the mouse ran away.

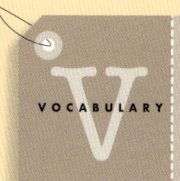

VOCABULARY

1. **bump into** v. ☞ ～にばったり出くわす
2. **paw** n. ☞ 手
3. **forgive** v. (forgive-forgave-forgiven) ☞ 許す

Two weeks later, the mouse heard the lion from far away.

He ran to the sound and found the lion in a net. Some hunters❶ had caught the large animal.

The mouse waited. When the hunters left to get their wagon,❷ he quickly began biting the net.

Soon, the net broke and the lion was free. The lion put the mouse on his back and ran into the forest.❸

When they stopped, the mouse said, "I told you I could help you one day."

The lion said, "I'm sorry I doubted❹ you. Now I realize there is greatness even in a small mouse."

VOCABULARY

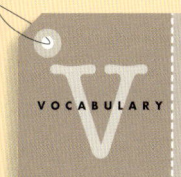

1. **hunter** n. ☞ 猟師
2. **wagon** n. ☞ 荷馬車
3. **forest** n. ☞ 森
4. **doubt** v. ☞ 疑う

The Lion and the Mouse **ライオンとネズミ**

訳：ライオンとネズミ

　ある日、一匹のネズミが、寝ていたライオンの手にうっかりぶつかってしまいました。ライオンは目を開けて、その大きな手をネズミに向かって伸ばしました。
　ネズミは言います。
「ごめんなさい！ 痛い目にあわせないで！」
　ライオンは、ネズミを食べてやろうとつまみ上げました。
　「お願い。許してください！」とネズミは泣きました。
「忘れずにいつか必ずあなたを助けますから」
　ライオンは笑ってたずねました。
「どうやって、ちっこいネズミが偉大なライオンさまを助けるっていうんだ？」
　「でも、笑わせてくれたから、放してやるか」
　ライオンがネズミを下に降ろすと、ネズミは走り去りました。

　２週間後、ネズミは遠くのほうでライオンの声がするのを聞きました。
　声のほうに走って行くと、ライオンは網の中。猟師たちがこの大きな動物を捕らえたのです。
　ネズミは待ちました。猟師たちが荷馬車を取りにその場を離れると、ネズミは素早く網をかじり始めました。
　すぐに網は破れ、ライオンは自由の身になりました。ライオンはネズミを背中に乗せ、森の中に駆け込みました。
　２匹が立ち止まったとき、ネズミは言いました。
「僕、言ったでしょ。いつか助けますって」
　ライオンは言いました。
「すまんな。信じてなかったよ。でも、もうわかった。ちっこいネズミも大したもんだってね」

The Goose and the Golden Eggs
アヒルと金の卵

124

Once there was a very poor [1] man. He was often hungry and his clothes were full of holes. He was very sad.

Then one day, he found a lovely goose [2] in the forest and took it home. The next morning, the poor man discovered a small golden egg under the goose. His face lit up with joy. [3]

"This is amazing!" [4] he shouted. He took the egg to the market and sold it. Then he used the money to buy food and clothes.

"Life is getting better," he said happily.

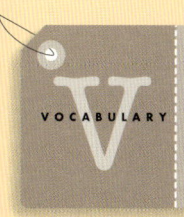

VOCABULARY

1. **poor** adj. ☞ 貧しい
2. **goose** n. ☞ アヒル
3. **joy** n. ☞ 喜び
4. **amazing** adj. ☞ 驚くべき、すごい

The goose changed the man's life. It laid ❶ a golden egg every morning. The man had no worries now, but he became greedy. ❷

"This goose must be bursting with golden eggs!" he thought. "I hate getting them so slowly."

Hoping to get rich faster, he killed the goose and cut it open with a knife. ❸ However, there was nothing special inside.

The man felt very stupid. "I could have been rich," he cried, "but I was greedy, and now I have nothing."

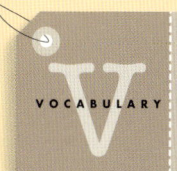

VOCABULARY	1. **lay** v. (lay-laid-laid) ☞ 卵を産む
	2. **greedy** adj. ☞ 欲張りの
	3. **knife** n. ☞ ナイフ

The Goose and the Golden Eggs **アヒルと金の卵**

訳：アヒルと金の卵

　昔、とても貧しい男がいました。いつもお腹を空かせ、服は穴だらけ。男はとてもみじめでした。

　そんなある日、森の中で男は美しいアヒルを見つけ、連れ帰りました。翌朝、貧しい男はアヒルの下に小さな金の卵を発見します。男の顔は喜びに輝きました。

「信じられない！」

　男は叫びました。男は、卵を市場に持って行き、売りました。そして、そのお金で食べ物と服を買いました。

「人生が上向いてきたぞ」

　男はうれしそうに言いました。

　アヒルは男の人生を変えました。アヒルは毎朝、金の卵を一つ生みました。男はもう何も心配がなくなりました。でも、欲張りになったのです。

「このアヒルには金の卵が詰まっているに違いない」

　男は思いました。

「ちまちま卵を取り出すのは面倒だ」

　男は、早く金持ちになりたくて、アヒルを殺し、ナイフで切り裂きました。でも、その中には何もありませんでした。

　男は、自分が愚かだったと感じました。

「金持ちになれたのに、欲を出してすべて失ってしまった」

　男は嘆きました。

Index

索引

a

admire	71
agree	59
amazing	125
apologize	31
ashamed	83
at the sight of	73
attack	102

b

beat	13
beg	67
bill	29
bite	42
bitter	95
bored	101
bridge	85
bump into	119

c

careful	42
careless	97
carry	59
clap	109
claw	54
clever	71
climb	49
comfortable	95
common	90
concern	95
confident	37
continue	37
cross	59
cry	114

d

dangerous	54
delicious	53
die	61
disappointed	29
donkey	83
doubt	121
dress	24

e

embarrassed	89
escape	17

f

fable	102
fall	79
fancy	71
farmer	76
fear	97
field	24
fool around	65
forest	121
forgive	119

free ········· 31

g

gather	65
grasshopper	65
generous	97
goose	125
gray	113
greedy	109 · 127
grow	76
growl	31

h

hare	35
hatch	76
healthy	89
hide	18
hill	23
honest	107
honey	53
hunter	121
hurry	41

i

| impossible | 35 |
| invitation | 29 |

j

| joy | 125 |

k

| king | 113 |
| knife | 127 |

l

lap	47
lap up	29
lay	127
lazy	83
leaf	41
lick	47
lioness	89
log	11

m

| make sense | 59 |
| middle | 61 |

n

nap	37
naughty	73
nectar	11
net	42
note	95
notice	67

o

once upon a time	23
original	107
overload	85

p

pack of	18
pass by	89
paw	119

please	114
pole	85
poor	125
proud	17
punish	13

r

race	35
reach	61
real	24
ride	61
roar	13

s

safe	41
scorpion	59
scratch	47
servant	47
shame on you	83
sharp	54
sheepskin	23
shine	97
shout	101
silly	114
sly	17
sniff	11
spill	79
stable	47
starve	67
stick	49
sting	59
stranger	109
suggest	65

t

tear	73
temper	13
tortoise	35
toss one's head	79
town	101
treat	49
truly	89
turn around	89

u

unhappy	113

v

valuable	90

w

wagon	121
welcome	31
well-known	102
wife	113
wizard	107
wonderful	53
wood	11
worth	90

y

yell	42

Live ABC

　株式会社 Live ABC は、台湾の e-Learning プログラムにおいてトップレベルの実績を誇っている大手出版社です。最先端の IT 技術と経験豊富な技術者と語学教師及び編集スタッフによって、インタラクティブマルチメディア語学学習教材の研究開発に取り組んでいます。
　現在、英語を筆頭に中国語、日本語、韓国語などの語学学習教材を、書籍や、CD-ROM、スマートフォン対応のアプリで提供しています。

ホームページ（英語）：http://www.liveabc.com

カバーデザイン	土岐 晋二（デザイン事務所フラクタル）
本文デザイン／ DTP	土岐 晋二（デザイン事務所フラクタル）
CD ナレーション	Jack Merluzzi
	Carolyn Miller
	城内 美登理

音読 CD BOOK ①
改訂版 やさしい英語で読む　イソップ物語　～ Aesop's Fables ～　BEST 20
平成 23 年（2011 年）　3 月 10 日発売　初版第 1 刷発行
令和 4 年（2022 年）　7 月 10 日　　　　第 4 刷発行
編　者　Live ABC
発行人　福田富与
発行所　有限会社　J リサーチ出版
　　　　〒 166-0002　東京都杉並区高円寺北 2-29-14-705
　　　　電話 03 (6808) 8801 (代)　FAX 03 (5364) 5310
　　　　編集部 03 (6808) 8806
　　　　http://www.jresearch.co.jp
印刷所　（株）シナノ パブリッシング プレス

ISBN978-4-86392-055-2　禁無断転載。なお、乱丁・落丁はお取り替えいたします。
Copyright © 2011 LiveABC Interactive Corporation.
Japanese translation copyright © 2011 J-Research Press. Japanese edition. All Rights Reserved.